A TRIP TO THE FUTURE

For the scientists, engineers, writers and artists of the future.
Go out and change the world! – M.B.

To imagine the future is a fascinating adventure – FAGOSTUDIO

BIG PICTURE PRESS

First published in the UK in 2020 by Templar Books,
an imprint of Bonnier Books UK,
The Plaza, 535 King's Road, London, SW10 0SZ

www.templarco.co.uk
www.bonnierbooks.co.uk

1 3 5 7 9 10 8 6 4 2

ISBN 978-1-78741-575-1

Edited by Ruth Symons and Joanna McInerney
Designed by Kieran Hood
Production Controller: Nick Read

Printed in China

A TRIP TO THE FUTURE

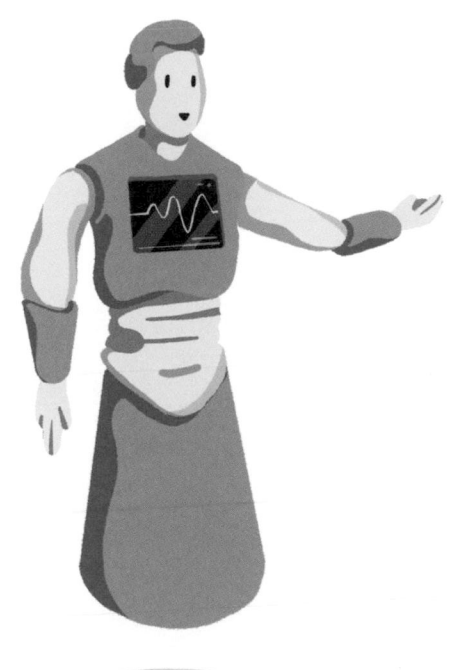

Moira Butterfield
and
FagoStudio

templar
books

CONTENTS

INTO THE FUTURE

Are you ready for super-smart homes and robot-friendly cities, parks in the sky, pollution-busting cars and planes, space hotels and schools on Mars? How about talking toilets, computerised trousers, pondweed burgers and trampolining on the Moon?

The future is coming! It's going to be full of exciting inventions, though we can't know for sure which ones will change our lives. However, the ideas in this book are based on science that people are working on today, so some of what you read is very likely to be used in years to come.

Life in the future is going to be full of science surprises. Perhaps you will help make some of them happen. Turn the page to step inside a world full of the fascinating, the peculiar, the practical and the unbelieveable... Step into the future!

THE HELPFUL ROBOT

Buy a hard-working buddy!

Robots are machines that can automatically carry out tasks again and again. House robots have already been invented to help with jobs such as cleaning and vacuuming. Helpful robots have been tried out in space, too. CIMON – short for Crew Interactive Mobile Companion – has been tested out on the International Space Station. It is a floating ball with a smiley face on its screen, and it can answer questions or play music. When it was first tested, it went wrong and kept playing the same tune over and over again. This shows there's still a lot of work to do before the robots shown here will be ready to buy for real.

SHOP

One day it might be normal to own house robots who will keep you company and help with tasks around the home. You might even visit a showroom like The Helpful Robot Shop to choose the latest handy robo-helper.

ROBOPOPPINS robo-babysitter
Good at playing games and answering difficult questions. Lullaby and homework apps available.

SIT-A-BOT robo-furniture
Automatically turns into a chair, sofa or bed platform. BOTTOM-TRAP WARNING: Do not sit on the robot when it is changing!

LESS-OF-A-MESS robo-housekeeper
Great for tidying up, ironing and folding. Includes attachments to dust, vacuum and mop.

ROBOWAG robo-pet
No feeding or pooping! Just charge up and go. Choose from a range of animals.

DATALICIOUS robo-chef
1,000,000 recipes available. Cameras and temperature probes guarantee food is perfectly cooked.

Robots are fitted with **sensors** and cameras to take in the world around them, and sometimes have a voice to respond to commands. The latest robots can learn to change the way they do their job, too. How much a robot can learn and change what it does depends on how many programming steps, called **algorithms**, it has been given. The algorithms are a set of instructions put into the robot using coding, the language of computers.

ARTIFICIAL INTELLIGENCE

- **AI** means Artificial Intelligence, and it's used in today's robots. An AI robot is programmed to do one type of job, such as vacuuming or cleaning.

- **AGI** means Artificial General Intelligence, and it might soon be possible. An AGI robot could do all sorts of different tasks and learn new ones.

- A **Superintelligent** robot would be smarter than humans, and could do anything. It doesn't exist yet, and it might not be a good idea anyway. It might tell you how to do your own jobs!

HOME, ~~SWEET~~ SMART HOME

Number 1 Future Street

In the future it will probably be normal to talk to your home and tell it how to work. You'll easily be able to change the way it looks, too.

One day it could be common for homes to be filled with sensors and computer controls that monitor and control everything, from the heating to the colour of the walls and the way the air smells. Even your toilet might get **smart**. It will know when to clean itself but it might also be able to analyse your poop to make sure you are healthy. It could give you some health tips, such as: "I can tell you need some vitamin C. Try eating an orange."

Future homes will be fuelled by sunlight, wind power or even **algae** – the green sludge that grows in ponds. A building in Germany is already being powered by micro-algae inside glass panels on its walls. Micro-algae love sunshine, which makes them grow. They turn into a bubbly goop that generates warmth for the house, and can be used to make **biofuel** or even food (see p 13).

Future houses are likely to be built more like Lego™ models, with bricks that slot together and walls that are easily moved around to change the shape of rooms. Homes might even be made from building material inspired by animals. Scientists have worked out how to grow material for bricks by using the same natural chemicals that an ocean animal – the abalone – uses to grow its shell. They're also hoping to make strong lightweight material by copying the tiny fibres inside reindeer antlers, and they've even made super-strong fabrics with the natural chemicals that a spider uses to spin web silk.

Voice command and reply technology will probably be much more common in future homes.

POWERED DRESSING
Textiles get technical

Clothes are already becoming smarter. Fabric can now be coated with a super-thin flexible film printed with light circuits called OLEDS (Organic Light-Emitting Diodes) which can light up clothes or change the colour of an outfit. With **voice recognition** controls built in, you'll soon be able to tell your clothes to change colour or glow in the dark!

One day you might be able to charge up a mobile phone with your trousers or watch a screen on your t-shirt. Designers have already found ways to generate battery power from fabric by weaving in sunlight-collecting fibres or tiny devices called **nanogenerators**, which make electricity whenever the fabric moves.

Solar fabrics can collect energy from sunlight to power gadgets.

Outfits could light up.

"Oops! I spilled some sauce. Quick, shirt. Change colour so it doesn't show!"

Future clothes will be made from surprising materials and it might be normal to hear someone talking to their outfit.

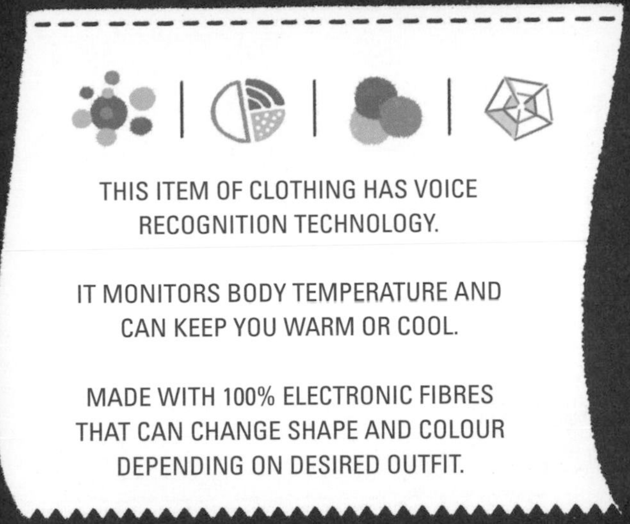

New eco-friendly fabrics are being invented and will probably become more common. For instance, **bioculture** clothes are made from yeast, fungi or algae, fermented in a vat of liquid to make material that is similar to leather. Leather can also be made from grape skins, mushrooms and even fermented tea. When bioculture clothes wear out they can be put on a compost heap, just like vegetable peelings.

THIS ITEM OF CLOTHING HAS VOICE RECOGNITION TECHNOLOGY.

IT MONITORS BODY TEMPERATURE AND CAN KEEP YOU WARM OR COOL.

MADE WITH 100% ELECTRONIC FIBRES THAT CAN CHANGE SHAPE AND COLOUR DEPENDING ON DESIRED OUTFIT.

Power generated by the movement of clothing might be able to charge gadgets.

Leather can already be made from fermented tea. It's called 'teather'.

"My coat is made from your tea!"

FUTURE CAFÉ

Best pondweed and sound cookies in town!

Step into the Future Café, where a robot waiter is ready to serve you food with plenty of science mixed in.

Insects, algae and lab food could help make healthier, cheaper food for everyone.

Food could be made by 3D printers and served by robots.

100% INSECT GOODNESS

"I think I'll have th pondweed burger."

Food is ordered via a digital menu in the Future Café.

Meat and milk can already be made in a science laboratory, and in the Future Café it will be normal to eat food made in a lab. In the café itself there might be 3D food printers. These can already mix and print simple food such as pasta dough. One day they might be able to mix together lots of tiny particles, called **nanoparticles**, to make more complicated food.

Starter
Nanoparticle snacks – choice of over 1,000 flavours.

Main Course
Pondweed burger and edible plate – made from top-quality pondweed.
Guaranteed no frogs.

Lab-tastic meatballs and mega-science milkshake.
All meat and milk fresh from a lab near you.

Dessert
Farm-fresh insect pancake.
Choice of insects: cricket, grasshopper, mealworm, fruit fly.

Sound cookie (with headphones) – choice of cookie sounds:
Extra-crunchy choir, chocolate symphony, chewy lullaby.

CHOOSE YOUR FOOD

NANOSNACK   PONDWEED   INSECT   LAB-GROWN

"The waiters are very switched-on here!"

Robo-waiters could run the restaurant.

We humans need to eat protein to help us survive. We get this from meat, eggs, dairy foods and nuts, but we can also get it from pondweed and seaweed, both types of algae. In the Future Café there will be lots of dishes made from algae. It can even be used to make edible plates.

As well as using taste buds on our tongues to enjoy food, it's been proved that listening to different sounds makes food taste sweeter or more bitter, depending on the tones you hear. In the Future Café, you might be given headphones and asked to listen to special soundtracks while you eat, to help make your food taste really great.

VISIT A DREAMWORLD

Pat unicorns and feed dinosaurs!

Would you like to visit a dreamworld where anything is possible, including fairies, unicorns and dinosaurs? Soon you'll be able to go to an imaginary world that won't just look real... it'll feel real, too.

Virtual reality, called VR for short, has already been invented. When you wear a VR headset it gives you the effect of standing in a 3D picture. In the future, this technology will be even more convincing because you'll be able to touch and feel your surroundings too. It's been discovered that tiny harmless electrical signals passed into your skin can fool your fingers into feeling textures that aren't really there. This same technique could help you feel a dinosaur's knobbly skin or a unicorn's soft mane!

Computer game designers have been experimenting with clothes that are fitted with sensors that can vibrate or squeeze into you to give you touch sensations. Using touch in this way is called **haptic technology,** and it could be built into an outfit to experience a VR world. Pressure and vibrations from your clothing will give you feelings connected to what you see, such as being tapped on the shoulder or having something crawl up your arm.

"It feels so soft!"

WELCOME TO THE BRAINTERNET!
Where think-power rules

Today lots of electronic devices can connect to each other, but what if they could connect to your brain, too? Welcome to the internet of the brain, sometimes called the **brainternet**!

When you have thoughts and feelings your brain generates lots of different electrical signals. If the signals could be measured and their meaning **decoded**, your thoughts and feelings could be transmitted to a computer and you could command it by simply thinking. In 2017, South African scientists sent brain signals to the internet for the first time, and some brain signals have been decoded and used to move robotic limbs (see p24). But decoding all human brain signals will take much longer and will need lots of study. The brainternet is definitely still in the future.

It's possible that tiny electrical pulses could one day be sent into your brain to make you feel different emotions. Someone could send you a feeling, not just a text or a voice message.

People might wear something that sends pulses to their brain, or they could have electronic chips implanted in their brains to make this happen. Do you think this is a good idea? Perhaps people won't want it, even if it gets invented!

Animals don't talk but they use body language and noises to tell us what they want and how they feel. Scientific work has already been done to decode the exact meaning of animal moves such as tail-wagging and noises such as meowing. Perhaps one day animal brain signals will also be decoded so we'll be able to tell what our pets are thinking, too.

"How wonderful! Thanks for connecting, dear."

i Gran. I had great time at e park today. sending you y feelings."

"Here is the drink you thought of, Sir."

Electronic **headgear** or a brain chip could connect your brain to other people's brains, to send and receive emotion signals, perhaps long-distance.

FUTUROPOLIS

Science on every corner

Over time, things are likely to look and sound very different in cities around the world, thanks to inventions being worked on today.

City building sites will look very different if concrete buildings are 3D-printed. There won't be any need for scaffolding or piles of concrete blocks. Instead a moving robotic arm will gradually build up the walls, piping on concrete layer by layer.

If skyscrapers become really high they will need to be curved to withstand strong winds.

Old buildings can be covered in a mesh skin.

"Don't the new farmscrapers look great?"

On the outside of buildings, we will soon be able to cover anything in spray-on solar paint, full of tiny light-sensitive dots that can gather sunlight for energy and perhaps be programmed to create adverts and artworks.

We won't have to demolish and rebuild old buildings either. Instead they can be covered with a transparent cocoon of self-cleaning mesh – a building skin that has already been invented by international architects LAVA. The new skin preserves the building, gives it a fresh update and allows for solar power and computer connections.

Hi-rise skyscrapers are popular in crowded cities because they save on space, and they are likely to get higher and higher with time. Super-tall skyscrapers will have to have curved shapes to soften the power of the wind whooshing round the building. This is a design idea called **vortex shedding.**

REAL-LIFE ROBOCOPS

Public officials such as police could be robots in future cities. The city of Dubai in the United Arab Emirates already has street police robots. You can report crimes or get information by using the robot's touchscreen. For now the robocops are more like helpful city guides.

Super-skyscrapers could be joined together by sky-rail links.

This building is being 3D printed.

Farmscrapers are skyscrapers that have indoor gardens and even fields full of crops. Belgian architect Vincent Callebaut is famous for designing futuristic farmscrapers that could soon be built in cities.

"At your cyber-service, Sir."

19

GET WELL SOON

Hospitals in the future might use new technology to help make you better if you're ill.

Take your nanorobots twice a day

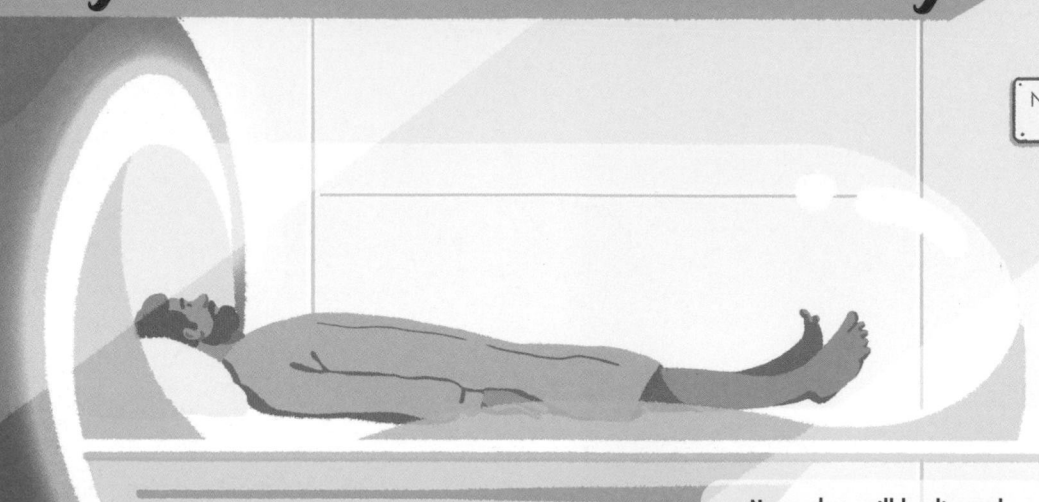

NANOROBOT ROOM

Bioactive paint could be used on walls to prevent infections.

"The nanorobots are sending me detailed information about your stomach, Mr Green. It all seems fine."

Nanorobots will be directed around the body by a doctor, perhaps using controls similar to a computer game.

Robot nurses could do simple checks on patients.

Personal robots could monitor each patient.

"Your teddy monitor says you are much better."

Bioactive bedclothes could prevent the spread of viruses and disease.

Hospitals are beginning to use more **bioactive material,** which contains additives that help fight bacteria and stop infections spreading. Patients can already have bioactive bandages but they might soon have bioactive sheets and curtains round their bed, too. Lots of objects in the hospital – such as tables, taps and doors – could also be covered in a bioactive coating.

Nanorobots are tiny particle-sized machines that can be built and programmed to carry out different jobs. All sorts of medical nanorobots are being developed to put inside the human body.

They are so small they can be injected into the bloodstream and guided through blood vessels to different parts of the body, where they can look for problems, deliver medicine or even fight bacteria.

Machines called **bioprinters** can already print 3D replacement body parts such as sections of skin and ears. They use human body cells as ink. It's not yet possible to print very complicated replacement body parts such as whole hearts and lungs, but one day it might be done.

The colour of hospital walls and lighting could be changed electronically to help make patients feel relaxed.

"We've printed a lovely new ear for Mrs Smith."

"I am Nurse ZX22A/8, but you can call me Z. How are you today?"

"I think we'll change the walls to a peaceful sunset colour."

A PARK IN THE SKY
Glowing trees and leaves that clean

Future parks could be very different to those we have in cities and towns today. They might be high above our heads, and could help us to save water and cut pollution.

Future city plans could include a network of parks on overhead bridges. These would save space, and humans and wild animals could use the green tracks to get safely around town. Old overhead railway lines have already been turned into sky parks in some of today's cities.

We know that some plants can absorb polluting gases from the air and poisonous substances from the soil, helping to clean their surroundings without being harmed themselves. These leafy cleaners will probably be planted more and more in parks around towns. Some types of palms are good air-cleaners, along with some species of rubber plants, ivy and ferns.

Scientists in the USA's Massachusetts Institute of Technology have found a way of injecting tiny light-emitting nanoparticles into plants, so they glow in the dark. They're called **nanobionic plants**. The nanoparticles were made by copying the chemicals used by glowing fireflies. One day the researchers hope to make glow-in-the-dark trees, which might even replace some street lighting.

Researchers have used satellite sensors to measure the levels of heat in modern cities. They found that lots of tree cover in a park or a street can significantly lower the temperature of the air, through shade and also the water the plants release through their leaves. Planting lots more trees could help city-dwellers to cope in extra-hot summers.

Glass domes could shelter parts of the park.

"I love it here. The air is really fresh."

There could be swings in the sky for those who dare!

Lots of wild animals make cities their homes around the world. Overhead parks will help them to live safely in the middle of town.

3D hologram park sculptures could change every day.

"Yesterday that hologram statue was a mermaid!"

Nanobionic plants could provide lighting at night.

Recycled water could be sprayed around the park when it's hot.

Visitors could use lifts to access the sky park.

RAINWATER HARVESTING

No rain will go to waste in the parks of the future. Large-scale rain collecting is called **rainwater harvesting**, when water is channelled down pipes and into hidden storage tanks. The stored water could be used to hydrate the park in warm weather, or during a dry patch. You might start seeing more mini rain gardens, too. These are bowls or troughs dug into the ground. They gather rainwater and channel it into a pond filled with plants that grow well in water and help to filter it.

Human + Robot =
HI-TECH HELP

The **cyborgs** are coming, but don't panic! Cyborgs are part-human and part-robot. In stories they're often super-strong bad guys, but in real life cyborg science is likely to be hugely helpful to humans.

Replacement robot parts such as hands and feet can already be attached to a human body, to help people with disabilities. They're called **bionic parts,** and they move by picking up signals made by someone's brain (see p16). They send their own signals back to the brain of the person wearing them, to give them a sense of touch. The connection between a bionic part and a human brain is called a **neural link,** and these are being made better and better by today's bionics engineers.

An **exoskeleton** is a robotic outer body suit designed to help someone move their limbs, perhaps to exercise a paralysed limb or make it easier to move a damaged body part as it gets gradually better. There are already exoskeleton parts for legs and arms, and full-body exoskeletons have been developed to help people with disabilities to move without having to use a wheelchair.

So far exoskeletons cannot replace wheelchairs altogether, as they have only been tested in laboratories. It's also very expensive to make exoskeletons or bionic body parts. However, in the future they could become much cheaper and more common.

"My bionic foot moves exactly like a real foot!"

Robot body attachments can also be used to give humans superpowers. For instance, exoskeletons could be worn to pick up heavy loads or run very fast. It's even possible that humans could one day decide to give themselves unusual bionic body parts, such as permanent wings!

"The exoskeleton sensors tell me you are getting stronger every day."

Exoskeleton suits can help someone to strengthen their bones and muscles.

"This bionic hand can do anything a real hand can do."

Signals can pass back and forth between the brain and a bionic body part.

25

SUPERSPORTS
Record-smashing science

With hi-tech equipment sports stars of the future could be smashing today's record achievements.

An exoskeleton arm sleeve could help this archer fire with extra strength.

With VR, athletes could be see[n] running against dinosaurs!

Digital goggles that show different scenes could one day help everyone to play sports in a virtual reality world (see p14). For instance, you could swim in hi-tech goggles that make the water in your local swimming pool look like a coral reef. With digital running goggles you could race against Olympic stars or perhaps even dinosaurs or aliens!

Special exoskeletons (see p24) could help athletes perform like superheroes in a sports stadium, perhaps even running as fast as horses or throwing for unbelievable distances. Digital eye lenses could also be fitted, so an archer or a target-shooter could see much further and more accurately than an ordinary person.

Drones could hold targets in the sky.

"BULLSEYE!"

EVERYONE WELCOME. SPACESUITS SUPPLIED. SAFETY NETS TO STOP YOU FLOATING OFF.

MOON TRAMPOLINE DAY

SPACE SPORTS

Space sports such as low-gravity trampolining or moon dust skiing could develop when humans visit other worlds.

Robot swimmers could challenge human ones.

Webbed hands and feet could be an advantage for swimmers.

Tiny oxygen-filled particles injected into swimmers could help them compete in long underwater races without having to come up for breath. They might even have surgically-altered webbed fingers and toes, too — like a duck or frog — to help them move faster through water. Humans might not beat swimming robots, though... Japanese robot designers have already made a robot called the Swumanoid, which mimics swimming strokes, so perhaps record-breaking swim-bots could soon appear in sports pools, too.

ANDROID SHOPPING MALL
Our androids are here to help

Some robots are **androids** – robots designed to look and behave just like humans. There are only a few android designs at the moment and they are easy to tell apart from humans because of how they move and speak. But will you be able to spot them as easily in the future? Visit the android-run shopping mall to find some.

The latest androids have realistic artificial skin made of silicon. It's stretchy, soft and marked all over with tiny indentations like human skin pores. It can be mixed with tiny **nanofibres** able to pick up and transmit electrical current, so the robot has a sense of touch and can sense if something is hot or cold. In the future, androids will have skin that feels warm like human skin, too.

It's not easy to make a robot body move like a human. Inventors are gradually adding in human-like touches such as blinking eyes and the movements we make when we breathe, but getting a robot to walk naturally is one of the toughest challenges yet to be solved.

There's a big problem with androids that look and move almost like humans, but not quite. Some humans don't like them and even feel afraid of them. Robot-builders refer to robots like this as being in 'the uncanny valley', and often prefer to design robots that look more like friendly toys. If androids are ever to blend in they will need to be incredibly realistic, or they might keep making humans feel uncomfortable.

Holographic information boards could help shoppers find what they are looking for.

HELPFUL ANDROIDS

Today's androids have more than 50 facial expressions and can even sing and play the piano, but they are nowhere near the androids in this future shopping mall. The androids will recognise the tone of your voice and the expressions on your face, so they can react naturally to you. Androids are being designed to help people, such as giving them information.

THE FUTURE SCHOOL

The school of the future might have robot help, and it could even be located on another planet. There will probably still be a teacher, though, and they're likely to be projecting pictures and information into the air in their classrooms.

With added robots and giant whales

Robot teaching assistants will be able to instantly spot anyone misbehaving in class... but they can also praise good behaviour, too.

Great work!

Teachers may soon be using an AR – **augmented reality** – device to project 3D images and information in front of their class. AR holograms will be helpful for learning all sorts of subjects. For instance, in a geography lesson an erupting volcano could appear right in front of the pupils, and in a nature lesson a whale could swim through the classroom!

Tests have shown that people learn better if they are taught by humans rather than robots or screen images. This may be because our brains have developed to copy and practise things we see other humans doing. It's how we learn as babies, just as other baby animals do in the wild. For that reason, robot teachers might not be a good idea, but we could still have robot classroom assistants.

If it becomes possible to implant a computer chip into the brain (see p17), will anyone need to learn anything ever again? Perhaps one day brain chips will help us learn, but it's more likely that humans will want to stay in control. That probably means schools won't be cancelled any time soon and children of the future will still have to do their homework!

"I am a hologram humpback whale from Earth, here to help you."

AR holograms will be connected to the internet and they'll be able to answer any questions and speak in any language.

"Today we will be learning about ocean animals."

The plastic we throw away lasts for centuries, and once it reaches the countryside and ocean it is a deadly danger to wildlife. One answer could be plastic-eating bacteria. They eat plastic by secreting an enzyme (a type of chemical) that dissolves it into separate ingredients that can be recycled into new products.

With the help of bacteria we can even turn poop into power. Some towns around the world are already recycling dog poop by giving it to bacteria to munch. The process is called **anaerobic digestion.** The bacteria make gas as they eat, which can be used to power electricity generators or even vehicles. Any leftover poop is made safe to use as fertilizer. Human poop can be treated the same way.

There are more and more clever ways of reusing things. For instance, a new type of material called **aerogel** is great for soaking up oil and petrol spills, and it can be made from discarded fruit. Banana peel, leftover citrus fruit and even cabbage leaves can be treated and then mixed with a type of silicon (found in sand and glass) to make the aerogel. It is lighter than air, safe for the environment and able to soak up lots of liquid.

Because it's so important to reuse the things we throw away, it's probably a good idea to stop calling it 'waste'. That way, we might all think harder about recycling it!

"Thanks for donating your old clothes and toys!"

We'll munch up your mush!

Recycling centres could use bacteria-munching technology to help break down rubbish.

RECYCLE HERE

It's vital that we do our best to recycle the things we use, to make the future a cleaner, safer place. Scientists are finding new ways to help, and their inventions might be used at recycling depots in the future.

...od waste can already be used
...to produce green electricity.

Plastic-dissolving bacteria could help
tackle pollution in the ocean.

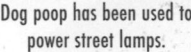
Dog poop has been used to
power street lamps.

FRUIT CHUTE

PLASTIC DESTROYER

DOG POOP DROP

Cars have already been built to run on
the gas from human poop. Engineers
think that poop from 70 average
homes could run a car for a year.

CALL THE SWARM!

All sorts of mini machine swarms will be helping us in the future, from drones to nanorobots that are too small see.

Your helpful mini friends are here

Mini drones (flying robots) can be made to act together in a big group, moving alongside each other like a shoal of fish. Swarms of tiny drones have already been used to create great sky displays at big events such as the Olympics. In the future they could be used as co-ordinated teams of mini workers, carrying out jobs such as spray-painting bridges and buildings.

Even tinier microscopic robots – **nanorobots** – can work in swarms, too (see p21 for more about them). They can be programmed to come together in a clump to plug tiny cracks in electronic circuits, for example. One day they could be used to fill cracks in the metal on bridges or plug damage on old buildings.

A special type of nanorobot called an assembler is capable of putting together molecules to build other nanorobots. It could even build copies of itself over and over again, to create its own swarm of nanorobots.

This swarm of drones will synchronise and work together to help repair the bridge.

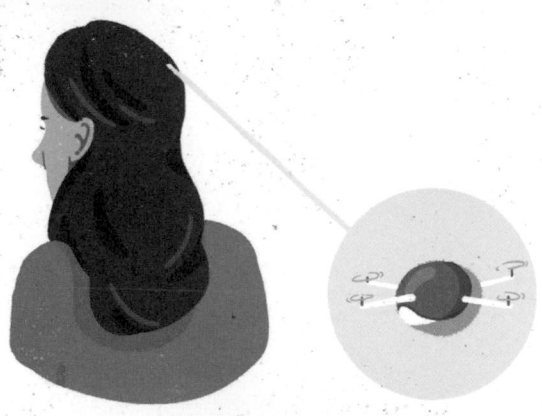

SWARM SIZES

Currently drones can be made about as small as paper clips. Most are slightly larger, about the size of an orange.

Nanorobots are so small they are measured in nanometres (one billionth of a metre) and micrometres (1 micrometre = 1000 nanometres). 75,000 nanometres could fit across one human hair.

Nanorobots come in lots of different shapes, such as tiny cubes, tubes or spheres. They range in size from around 100 nanometres to 10 micrometres.

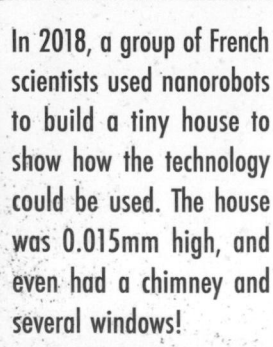

In 2018, a group of French scientists used nanorobots to build a tiny house to show how the technology could be used. The house was 0.015mm high, and even had a chimney and several windows!

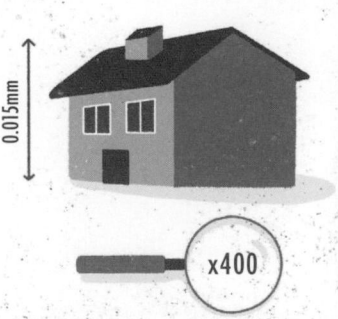

0.015mm

x400

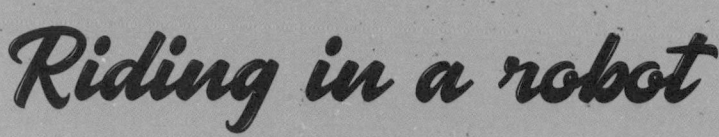

ROAD TO THE FUTURE
Riding in a robot

"The driver of Car 3 is feeling confident – her car has gone blue!"

Hovering racing cars could go much faster than cars with tyres that drag on the road.

A robot racing car could drive itself on some sections of the track, with drivers taking over on the bends to show their skills.

"We look set to complete the final lap in record time!"

"Oh, no! It looks like the driver of Car 5 is in trouble. He's stopped in the pit to recharge."

Electric cars could be recharged at stations, or by driving over WiFi induction mats fitted in the road. These would send pulses of power automatically to the car.

It's hard to predict what transport will be like in the future because there are many different ideas. Engineers are currently working on projects that could change everyday cars and racing cars forever.

Future cars will be like robots you can sit in. They'll be able to drive themselves, change shape to fit into parking spaces and even change colour. An exciting idea has been suggested for future motor races – cars that will change colour to match the emotions of their drivers. Watching fans will then be able to tell if their favourite driver is excited, tense or disappointed as they race round at top speed!

It's possible that cars might levitate and hover in the future, using magnetic forces underneath them to stay off the ground. Without tyres dragging on a road they could go much faster than today's cars. For that to happen, however, the road they drive on will need to be magnetic, too.

Vehicles of all kinds will soon run on electricity rather than fuels that pollute the air. The power could come from a battery or a hydrogen fuel cell, which mixes hydrogen gas with oxygen from the air to make electricity. Already some cars can run on biofuel made from algae or even gas made from sewage (see p32), and there may be other amazing eco-friendly new fuel ideas to come.

FLOATSVILLE 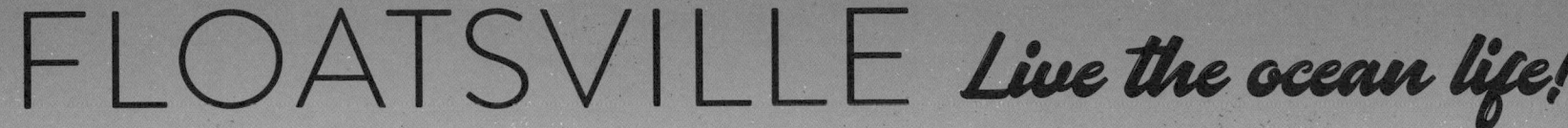 *Live the ocean life!*

Coastal cities could soon get floating neighbourhoods on the ocean. With more space needed in cities, and sea levels rising around the world, engineers and architects are looking at new ways for us to live on water and perhaps cope with serious flooding caused by climate change.

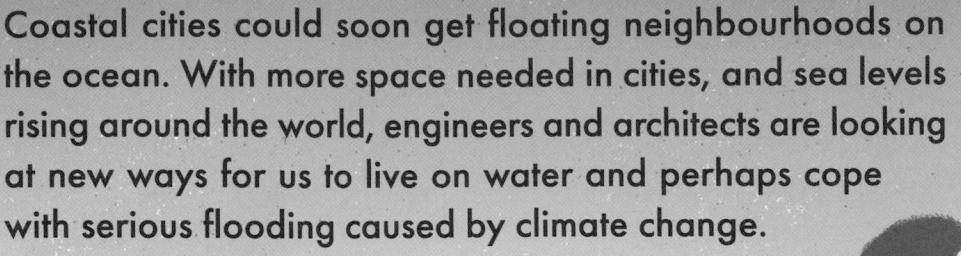

Wind and tidal power generators could run the platforms.

Aquatic engineers have been making plans to build homes, ports, farms and parks on floating concrete platforms tethered in shallow water. The platforms could be fitted together to create a mega-island protected from bad weather by a barrage built around it. There would have to be protection from sea sickness, too!

If we build floating cities, we need to ensure that they help the environment, not harm it. The new ocean islands could have their power provided by wind turbines, with blades spun round by the wind out in the breezy ocean. They could also use tide turbines to convert the movement of water into power.

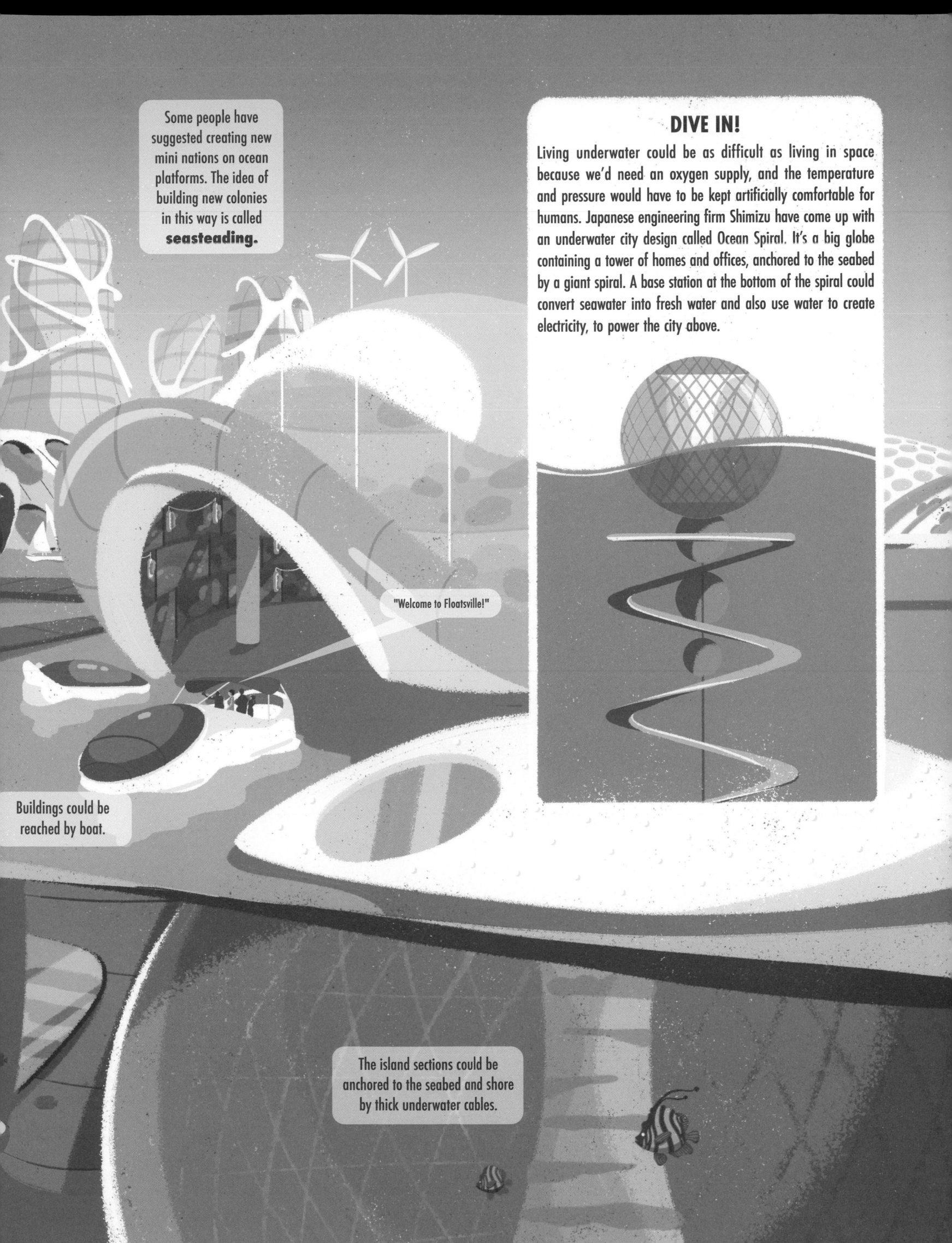

Some people have suggested creating new mini nations on ocean platforms. The idea of building new colonies in this way is called **seasteading.**

DIVE IN!

Living underwater could be as difficult as living in space because we'd need an oxygen supply, and the temperature and pressure would have to be kept artificially comfortable for humans. Japanese engineering firm Shimizu have come up with an underwater city design called Ocean Spiral. It's a big globe containing a tower of homes and offices, anchored to the seabed by a giant spiral. A base station at the bottom of the spiral could convert seawater into fresh water and also use water to create electricity, to power the city above.

"Welcome to Floatsville!"

Buildings could be reached by boat.

The island sections could be anchored to the seabed and shore by thick underwater cables.

MAMMOPHANT SAFARI

Science is already being used to help animals survive or rescue them from the edge of extinction. What if it could also help bring versions of extinct animals back?

Every cell in an animal's body contains its DNA codes. DNA is like a list of ingredients that controls how a living thing looks and grows. Sections of DNA are called genes, and all the genes together are called a genome. It's possible to get DNA from one animal and mix it with DNA from a similar species to get a new type of animal. That's how a new version of the woolly mammoth could one day reappear back in the mammoth's home in Siberia, Russia.

To get DNA from an extinct animal you must first find some preserved body parts. In 2013, a baby woolly mammoth found frozen in ice provided DNA for the woolly mammoth species, which died out around 40,000 years ago. It's 99% similar to elephant DNA, and it's possible that by mixing the two together scientists could give a mother elephant a woolly mammoth baby. The baby would be a cross between the two – a mammophant. Future tourists might even go on a mammophant safari.

Woolly mammoths are back!

Drones could monitor the mammophants to ensure their health.

Vets could download helpful information from mammophant drones.

"The herd is in good shape today."

Could dinosaurs be brought back using their DNA, perhaps mixed with a bird or a modern reptile? Probably not. They died out 66 million years ago and DNA doesn't usually last that long. In fact, the oldest DNA found so far came from a horse who lived 700,000 years ago... but who knows what other animals we might be able to bring back to life?

DRONES TO THE RESCUE

Science can help animal conservation in today's world. For instance, drones can be used to monitor wild animals without disturbing them. A drone called the SnotBot has been used to check on the health of whales. The SnotBot hovers above a whale and collects some of the goocy snot it blows out when it resurfaces. The snot can give researchers lots of medical information about the whale.

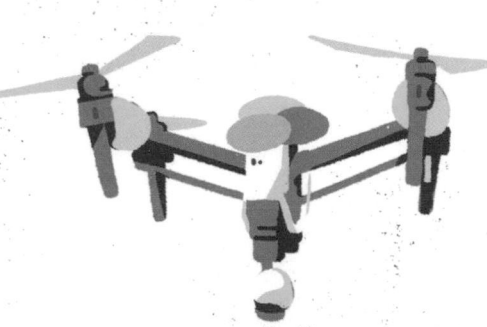

Existing highly-endangered animals may be saved by DNA bio-engineering, too. These Siberian cranes are now very rare. Their DNA could be gathered and used to breed new versions.

PLANET-FRIENDLY PLANES

Fly fast and clean!

Today's aeroplanes burn jet fuel that causes air pollution, so plane designers are hard at work trying to make flying more planet-friendly.

Planes that fly short distances can run on electricity rather than jet fuel, but at the moment it's hard to make a battery that will provide enough power for a long flight. In 2016, a Swiss plane called *Solar Impulse II* became the first plane to fly round the world on solar power, but it had to make lots of stops along the way. Engineers might find ways to use hydrogen fuel cells (see p37) as well as solar cells on the wings to capture the power of sunlight.

Swivelling engines can be used for taking off and landing vertically.

These bumpy wings were inspired by humpback whales.

Future planes probably won't be the same shape as planes are now. They could be much sleeker, so they slip more easily through the air. One new wing design isn't smooth, though. It copies the bumpy front edge of a humpback whale flipper. Scientists discovered that the bumps change the way water flows round the flipper, helping the whale to travel more easily through the ocean. Similar bumps work the same way on planes pushing through the air.

Scientists are working on ways to make damaged aeroplane wings heal themselves, just as your body can heal a small cut in your skin by making a scab. Tiny **microcapsules** inside the wing material could bleed chemicals that plug any small cracks or dents. Materials that heal themselves in this way could become much more common and help machines to last longer.

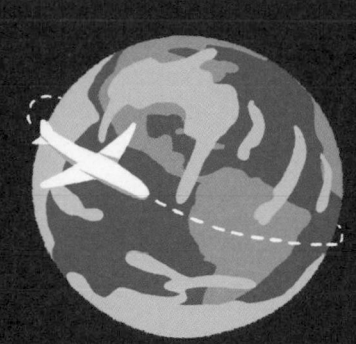

RACE THROUGH SPACE

Some planned planes are more like rockets travelling in space above Earth's atmosphere. Here they won't be slowed down by air pushing against them, and it's possible they could fly round the world in just a couple of hours, going at speeds of up to 6,115kph. Today's jet airlines cruise at around 930kph.

A solar-powered plane would need wide wings to fit on lots of solar cells.

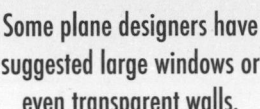
Some plane designers have suggested large windows or even transparent walls.

Delta wing planes, shaped like triangles, could become more common because they are very streamlined.

SOLAR SAILING
Sun-riding into space

All kinds of plans are being made to explore space in the future, including sending robot sailors off on missions carried along by sun-powered sails.

A **solar sail** is a large thin piece of reflective material attached to a small robot spacecraft. It is designed to catch the sun's rays out in space which help to propel it forward, the way a yacht sail is pushed by the wind.

A solar sail will take a while to start moving fast, but over a few years it could eventually reach very high speeds, perhaps even 240,000kph or more. That makes it ideal for exploring distant space. For instance, a solar sail-powered probe might be able to reach the dwarf planet of Pluto in around five years, less than half the time it has taken probes up to now. The sail could be sped up or slowed down by changing its angle to the sun's rays.

It will take a long, long time for solar sail communications to get back to Earth from far away in deep space. Their return messages might be monitored by the grown-up children or even grandchildren of the scientists who first built them.

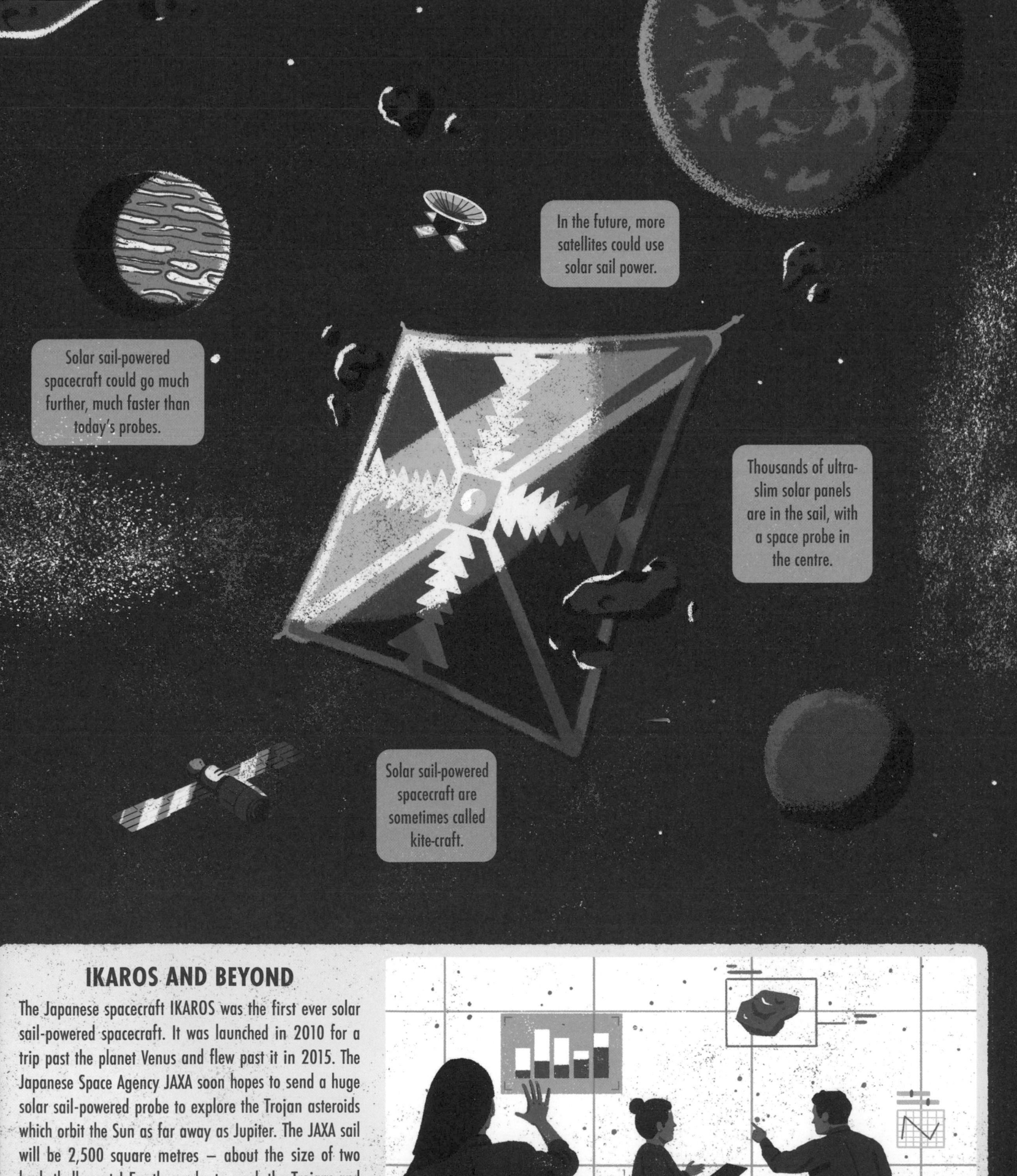

In the future, more satellites could use solar sail power.

Solar sail-powered spacecraft could go much further, much faster than today's probes.

Thousands of ultra-slim solar panels are in the sail, with a space probe in the centre.

Solar sail-powered spacecraft are sometimes called kite-craft.

IKAROS AND BEYOND

The Japanese spacecraft IKAROS was the first ever solar sail-powered spacecraft. It was launched in 2010 for a trip past the planet Venus and flew past it in 2015. The Japanese Space Agency JAXA soon hopes to send a huge solar sail-powered probe to explore the Trojan asteroids which orbit the Sun as far away as Jupiter. The JAXA sail will be 2,500 square metres — about the size of two basketball courts! For the probe to reach the Trojans and return, it needs to be big to generate plenty of solar power. If the JAXA mission is launched in the 2020s it should return to Earth in the 2050s, carrying asteroid samples, which may help us to understand more about the birth of our Solar System.

SPACE ELEVATOR
Moon lift now departing!

If you want to go to the Moon any time soon you'll need to blast into space in a rocket full of expensive – and dangerous – fuel. But in the far future, you might be able to hop on board a space elevator instead, for a cheaper, safer journey.

Before a space elevator can be built, there are some science problems to solve. The elevator's cables will have to be made of material that is stronger and lighter than anything we have today, so scientists will need to invent a new kind of molecule to make them. Tiny tube-shaped molecules called **carbon nanotubes** were made this way in the 1990s. They are 100 times stronger than steel and 10 times lighter – but the space elevator cables will need to be stronger and lighter still.

We'll also need to find a way of protecting the elevator from satellites, spaceship junk and asteroids floating out in space. These could perhaps be diverted away using a 'laser broom' – a laser beam aimed from Earth. Perhaps one day you will help to solve questions like this, so people can zip up to the Moon!

Cables could connect the base station to a station in orbit around Earth. Further cables will go to the Moon.

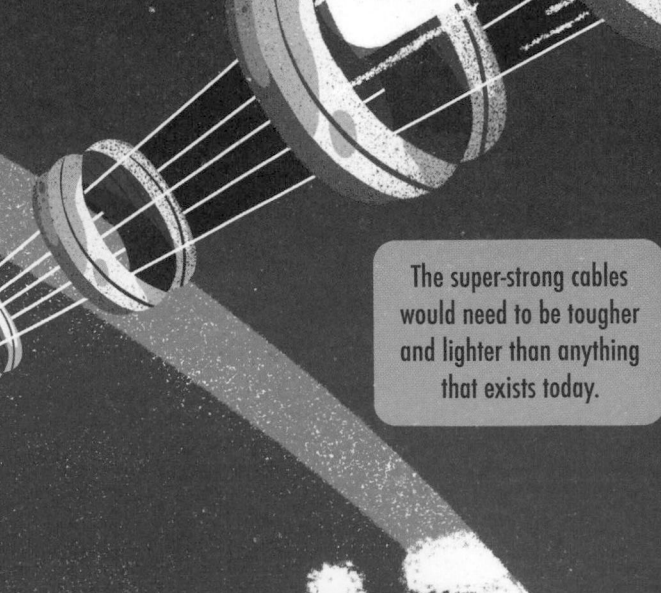

The super-strong cables would need to be tougher and lighter than anything that exists today.

Your journey would begin at a base station on Earth – a giant tower higher than any building in the world. The base might be on a floating platform so it can be moved away from major weather events, such as storms.

The midway station would be a place for people to stretch their legs before boarding a second space elevator. Next stop, the Moon!

Electric pods could zip up and down the cables at top speed, carrying people and cargo.

If the elevator could travel at around 200kph, the journey would take eight or nine days one-way. There would be beds on board, TVs for entertainment and windows for amazing space views!

COSMIC HOTEL

Holidays get rocket-powered

Would you like to stay in a hotel orbiting round Earth? It could happen one day... but will it be a relaxing trip or your worst off-world nightmare?

Plans are already being made for a space station hotel that will orbit the Earth, but it might not be an easy trip. You'd have to get used to floating around in zero gravity on-board and we know from the experiences of astronauts that this might cause space sickness, which is similar to sea sickness. It could take you a few days to get over it at the start of your holiday.

To make artificial gravity for guests, the space hotel would have to spin round. That would be difficult to design, but perhaps to begin with, a separate tethered section of the hotel could spin, to provide a running track or a swimming pool. Without artificial gravity the pool's water would float around in one big blob!

On Earth, our atmosphere protects us from dangerous radiation coming from the Sun. There's much less protection for a craft orbiting in space, so the hotel would need a strong outer radiation shield to protect the hotel staff and guests. Occasionally, an intense burst of radiation called a solar flare erupts from the Sun, and that will pose extra danger. The hotel would need solar flare storm shelters where guests and staff could go if there's a solar flare alert. In 2017, astronauts on the International Space Station had to do just this, hiding in a shelter during a massive solar flare.

Guests could float in an indoor swimming pool that spins round hotel to create artificial gravity

Trained guests could book a spacewalk activity.

Guests would get amazing views! If they were orbiting the Earth every 90 minutes, 400km high (the same orbit as the International Space Station), they would see 16 sunrises and sunsets every 24 hours.

MINE AN ASTEROID
Discover space-gold and water

Could asteroids be hiding metals worth trillions, or a precious water supply? Plans are being made to find out, and perhaps mine them for their riches.

ASTEROID WATER

This Rock drink...

ROCKS!

DON'T GO THIRSTY IN SPACE

SPACE WATER

Some asteroids are likely to contain frozen water, which could be melted by heated probes fired into the surface. The water would become steam that could be captured, turned back into liquid and sent to spacecraft for humans to drink. It could also be split into hydrogen (fuel for spacecraft) and oxygen (for astronauts to breathe in space).

A space ferry could transport loads of asteroid rock back to Earth.

A robotic mining craft could be attached to an asteroid. The rock would be processed inside the craft.

There are many asteroids that pass close enough to Earth for spacecraft to reach. Robot probes are already being sent to check up on some of them. It's possible they could contain metals that are rare and expensive on Earth, such as gold or platinum.

It would be very difficult to set up a mining camp on the surface of an asteroid, since gravity would be very weak and everything that wasn't fixed down would float away. Scientists at Vienna University in Austria have suggested solving this by building a space mine inside the middle of an asteroid. Robots would do the dangerous work in the mine and the metals found would be sent back to Earth on-board spacecraft.

Asteroids would have to be very carefully chosen for mining. Some are solid, but others are made of rubble which would be very unstable to land on and mine.

Plans are being made to send robot probes to catch a small asteroid, and either tow it back to orbit the Moon (where it could be reached by astronauts) or even bring it back to Earth to study.

Robot mining machines could work inside the asteroid.

Space probes could analyse an asteroid to see if it is worth mining.

COME TO MARS
Colony 1 needs you... but you must be brave

By the year 2150, humans could be setting up the first colony on Mars.
It's the nearest planet to Earth and it could be a useful base for asteroid mining.
But life there won't be easy...

It will take months to get to Mars, so visitors will have to be prepared for a long trip and take everything they might need with them. When they arrive, they'll face many dangers. The atmosphere on Mars is deadly to humans: it's bone-chillingly cold and huge dust storms rage for months. No one will be able to go outside without breathing equipment and a protective spacesuit.

Workers could use mini spacecraft to travel between Mars and a base on one of its moons.

Martian spacesuits are already being tested out on Earth. They will need to be super-tough and protective.

There might be less risk from radiation and meteor strikes on a base set up on one of Mars's two moons.

Greetings from Mars

Perhaps visitors will holiday on Mars one day! It won't look like Earth, but it will be an amazing place to stargaze and there are huge canyons, volcanoes, caves and craters to explore.

Spaceships for going home could be built on Mars, using parts delivered from Earth.

Dust storms would be common.

Robots could do most of the outdoor work, such as cleaning the solar panels used to power the base.

Modules would house leisure areas and indoor farms for growing food.

Buildings will probably have sections called modules, with tunnels between them. Inside there will be rooms to sleep and work, and greenhouses for growing plants under lights. The buildings will need to be covered in shields to protect the humans inside them from high levels of radiation and meteor strikes (Mars gets 200 times more meteor strikes than we do on Earth).

TERRAFORMING TIME
Refurbing the red planet

Would it be possible to turn Mars into a more Earth-like planet, so it would be easier to live on? The idea of changing a planet in this way is called 'terraforming'. Scientists have been coming up with theories on how it might be done.

Pools and streams could be created using melted Martian ice. Fish eggs could be hatched to provide food and fertilise the water, which could nourish plants.

Because of low gravity on Mars, inhabitants might have to do lots of bone and muscle-strengthening exercises every day.

Terraforming Mars would mean making its atmosphere more similar to Earth's, with plenty of oxygen so humans could breathe. It would also mean making it warmer and providing fresh water and plant life on the surface. It would be incredibly difficult to do this across the whole planet. However, with future technology, it might be possible to do this to a small section.

Earth has a thick atmosphere – a blanket of gases wrapped around it. Mars has a very thin atmosphere that would be difficult to alter overall. Any terraforming would have to take place under giant domes or wide roofs stretched over Martian valleys, with an Earth-like atmosphere and water supply created inside. The idea of making a habitat within a giant protective roof is called paraterraforming.

A comfortable temperature could be kept inside.
Outside it would be -60°C on average!

Mars's soil could be enriched with microbes and nutrients brought back from Earth.

An experiment has already been planned to see if oxygen-making bacteria can live on Mars. The bacteria will be **extremophile**, which means they can live in extreme temperatures and total darkness. If they survive, it's possible that oxygen farms could one day be created, full of bacteria-making oxygen that could be used to create an artificial atmosphere beneath a roof. For the experiment, bacteria will be sealed inside a canister, taken up to Mars by robot probe and fixed onto the planet's surface.

IN THE SPACE GARDEN

With sprouting space-seeds!

It would be hard to transport fresh food from Earth to a faraway space colony, so indoor space gardens will be needed to grow supplies.

We know from farms on Earth that crop plants can grow indoors as long as they are provided with water, nutrients and light. Instead of soil they can be grown **hydroponically** (with their roots in a watery gel) or **aeroponically** (with their roots hanging in misty air). Food crops such as lettuces and tomatoes could be grown inside space colonies, up the sides of walls or in plant towers to save room. Astronauts have already grown salad crops on space stations, so we know that space plants can thrive.

Some plants, such as fruit trees, need soil to grow in. It's now possible to make artificial soil by adding chemicals to recycled waste, and that's good news for space colonies of the future. Soil would be very heavy to carry from Earth, but scientists hope to mix chemicals with minerals found on the Moon or Mars, to create space soil on-site.

Back on Earth we have around 1,400 seed banks, which are rather like plant libraries. Examples of the world's seeds are safely stored there, dried and frozen, to replace any wild plants that might die out in the future. One day there could be seed banks out in space, orbiting Earth or set up on Mars to ensure that space colonies have replacement plants.

Scientists are working on ways to genetically modify plants to produce useful medicine-making chemicals, so space colonists could make medicine from plants as well as food. University of London researchers altered the DNA of a lettuce to produce a drug that treats bone weakening, a problem for astronauts on long rocket trips.

Space colonists could grow plants to make their own medicine.

A 'soft hand' robot would be able to do delicate jobs, such as taking plant cuttings.

THE FUTURE OF SCIENCE

Let's be brilliant!

Science could help us to do lots of amazing things in the future, but will it be used for good or bad? It's up to us.

We have seen in this book some amazing developments that could help humans in the future, from advances in medicine to super-smart homes. But if we are going to live alongside robots, it might be helpful to come up with some rules so that we can establish good relationships with each other.

RULES FOR ROBOTS

A scientist and author called Isaac Asimov once wrote a short story that included a set of rules for robot makers, to make sure they programmed their inventions well. The story rules have become famous in the world of science.

1. A robot must not injure a human or, through doing nothing, allow a human to be harmed.

2. A robot must obey humans unless their orders conflict (clash) with Rule 1.

3. A robot must protect itself as long as this does not conflict with Rules 1 and 2.

Get thinking...

Get ready...

Get inventi

Here comes
THE FUTURE!

RULES FOR US

Here are four ideas from the author of this book for future science rules. Do you agree or disagree with them?

1. HELP THE PLANET

Hopefully we will create new inventions that won't damage our planet and, very importantly, they could help us to stop polluting Earth and even reverse pollution that has already happened.

2. BE FAIR TO EVERYONE

Lots of future science will depend on computer programs written by humans. It's important that the programs don't discriminate against different kinds of people. Robot machines must be programmed to act fairly to everyone.

3. TALK ABOUT SCIENCE IDEAS

It's important that we talk about science ideas and get the chance to decide if we want them. Is there something in this book that you don't like the sound of? Why do you think it might be a bad idea? Make sure you get your say by talking about the things you have read or heard might happen in years to come.

4. ANYTHING IS POSSIBLE

Do you have your own incredible invention idea? Perhaps it sounds impossible at the moment, but in a few years it could become real. One day you might make it happen! There's lots to look forward to – and maybe to help with – in the future!

GLOSSARY

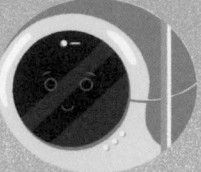

Aerogel – A super-light gel. Ordinary gel would contain liquid, but in aerogel it's replaced by gas.

Aeroponic – Growing plants with their roots in misty air instead of in soil.

AI – Short for Artificial Intelligence. A machine that can perform human-like tasks.

AR – Augmented Reality. An AR device projects 3D images and information into the air.

Algae – A green sludgy organism that grows in water. It can be made into fuel or fabric and is used in manufactured foods.

Algorithm – A set of instructions written in coding and used in a computer programme.

Anaerobic digestion – When bacteria feed on plant or animal matter and break it down into chemicals and gases that can be used as fuel.

Android – A robot designed to look and behave like a human.

Aquatic – Relating to water, 'aquatic' can mean anything which lives, grows or is carried out in water.

Bioactive material – Material such as fabric or paint containing additives to help fight bacteria.

Bioculture fabric – Fabric made from fermented yeast, fungi or algae.

Biofuel – Fuel made from plant or animal material.

Bionic parts – Replacement body parts that move by picking up a signal from the wearer's brain.

Bioprinter – A machine that prints 3D body parts using human cells as ink.

Brainternet – The idea of a brain sending and receiving signals to and from the internet.

Carbon nanotube – Also known as a CNT, these are tiny tubes made of carbon molecules. They are 100 times stronger than steel.

Cyborg – A human with added robot parts.

Decode – To work out a coded message.

Exoskeleton – A robotic outer body suit.

Extremophile – A microorganism that can thrive in extreme conditions.

Farmscraper – A skyscraper with lots of indoor gardens for growing crops.

Haptic technology – Sensors that vibrate or squeeze to give someone a touch sensation.

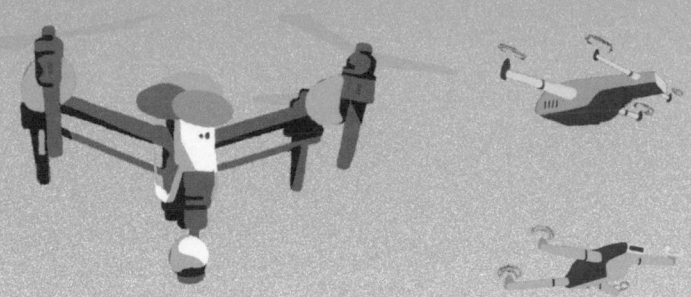

Headgear – An item worn on the head. In the future we may use more SMART headgear, which will feature technology such as sensors to monitor brain activity and aid communication.

Hydroponic – Growing plants in a watery gel instead of soil.

Microcapsule – A very tiny capsule used to transport particles.

Nanobionic plant – A plant containing light-emitting particles to make it glow in the dark.

Nanofibre – A type of fibre that is so thin it measures only a few nanometres in diameter. A nanometer is one billionth of a metre.

Nanogenerator – A tiny device that can generate energy when it is squeezed or vibrated.

Nanoparticle – Tiny particles too small to see with the human eye.

Nanorobot – Tiny particle-sized machines programmed to carry out a task.

Neural link – A connection between a bionic (machine) body part and a human brain.

Rainwater harvesting – Collecting rainwater to recycle.

Seasteading – The act of creating a permanent offshore settlement, known as a seastead.

Sensor – A device which detects or measures things and sends the data to a computer system.

Smart – Fitted with sensors connected to a computer system.

Solar sail – A large flat piece of material containing solar cells that catch sunlight to power a spacecraft.

Superintelligent – The word for a machine that could easily outperform even the brainiest human.

Terraforming – Changing a planet's landscape and atmosphere.

Voice recognition – When a machine responds to the commands of a human voice.

Vortex shedding design – A curvy design for a high skyscraper, to soften winds that swirl around the building.

Virtual reality – VR for short. The effect of standing in a 3D picture.

Wind turbine – A set of blades spun round by the wind, powering an electricity generator.

INDEX

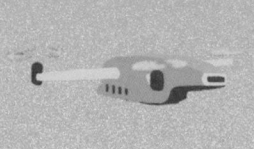

CREDITS

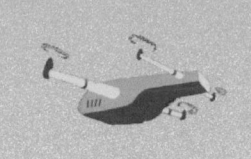

The predictions made in this book are the author's own selection, interpreted in their own way by the book's artists, but we have taken into account the comments of a range of impressively helpful experts in their field. With very many thanks to:

Dr Rob Wortham BSc (Hons), MEng, PhD, CEng, CITP, MIET, FBCS
Teaching Fellow in Robotics & Autonomous System,
Department of Electronic & Electrical Engineering, University of Bath, UK

Martin Parsons
Head of Studio, Centre for the Analysis of Motion, Entertainment Research and Applications,
University of Bath, UK

Cas Smith
Biological engineer, materials scientist and Director of Partnerships at Biofabricate
www.biofabricate.co

Dr Adelina Ilie
Reader, Centre for Nanoscience and Nanotechnology, Department of Physics,
Bath University, UK

Allison Kaye Harvey RLA, ASLA
OJB Landscape Architecture, Philadelphia, USA

Dr Alexandra E Sexton
Human geography postdoctoral researcher, Wellcome Trust 'Livestock, Environment and People' (LEAP) project, Oxford Martin School, Oxford University, UK

Pipistrel, Slovenia
www.pipistrel-aircraft.com

ABOUT THE AUTHOR

MOIRA BUTTERFIELD is an internationally-successful author of children's non-fiction and picture books. Her work has featured on the UK school curriculum and been commended by the US Library of Congress. She aims to add originality and fun to all her projects, to get her young readers engaged in the amazing world around them. Moira also blogs on children's books and occasionally runs creative festival workshops. She lives in Somerset, UK, where she is usually to be found exploring on her bicycle.

ABOUT THE ARTISTS

FAGOSTUDIO is one girl and two boys, six hands and three brains, paper, pencils, computer mice, damaged keyboards and shelves, often too tight deadlines and sometimes bugged software. Having worked together during their studies, the studio took form in a small workshop at Voltaire Street in Nantes, France. Attached to the peaceful and culturally rich city, the studio is now based in the creative district named 'Les Olivettes'.